Welcome to Life!

Teaching God's Word
to the Child in the Womb

"You saw me before I was born.
Every day of my life was recorded in your book.
Every moment was laid out before a single
day had passed." (Psalm 139:16 NLT)

Phyllis Nicholas and Anne Marie Wilson

ISBN 978-1-0980-9478-2 (paperback)
ISBN 978-1-0980-9480-5 (hardcover)
ISBN 978-1-0980-9479-9 (digital)

Christian Faith Publishing
832 Park Avenue
Meadville, PA 16335
www.christianfaithpublishing.com

Printed in the United States of America

Introduction

It is our prayer this book will bless you and your child or children in the womb as you read this book to them before birth. We also pray that you come to know the great love our heavenly Father has for the child in the womb and for each one of us.

This book is dedicated to the unborn child in the womb and to those yet to be born in Christ.

Phyllis Nicholas and Anne Marie Wilson

You saw me before I was born. Every day of my life was recorded in your book. Every moment was laid out before a single day had passed. (Psalm 139:16 NLT)

And you must think constantly about these commandments I am giving you today. You must teach them to your children and talk about them when you are at home or out for a walk; at bedtime and the first thing in the morning. Tie them on your finger, wear them on your forehead, and write them on the doorposts of your house! (Deuteronomy 6:6-9 TLB)

My dearest child in the womb,
My precious little one.
I am your Creator and Heavenly Father
and I am so happy that your life has now begun.

You made all the delicate, inner parts of my body and knit them together in my mother's womb. Thank you for making me so wonderfully complex! It is amazing to think about. Your workmanship is marvelous—and how well I know it. You were there while I was being formed in utter seclusion! (Psalm 139:13-15 TLB)

With your conception and even before,
I wanted to give you the best,
so, I made plans to give you a
life filled with joy, peace, and rest.

For I know the plans I have for you," declares the LORD, "plans to prosper you and not to harm you, plans to give you hope and a future. (Jeremiah 29:11 NIV)

So, listen to my words and stay very close to me,
then all things will work out for your good,
this I guarantee.

And we know that God causes everything to work together for the good of those who love God and are called according to his purpose. (Romans 8:28 NLT)

You were created by me,
so, you're not a mistake.
For you, my precious child,
are the icing on my cake.

So God created human beings in his image. In the
image of God he created them. He created them male
and female. (Genesis 1:27 NCV)

Of all my created works
that I long ago told,
You, my dear child,
are more valuable
than silver or gold.

…he who touches you touches the apple of his eye… (Zechariah 2:8 ESV)

I even created the birds and the trees,
but you, my dear love,
are greater than these.

So do not be afraid; you are worth more than many sparrows. (Matthew 10:31 NIV)

So remember, my little child, in the womb,
my love for you is very deep and always true,
that I even sing heavenly songs
over you.

The Lord your God is with you; He is mighty to save. He will take great delight in you, he will quiet you with his love, he will rejoice over you with singing. (Zephaniah 3:17)

GOD
is
LOVE

I am the Lord God.
whose love for you will never cease.
So never forget my word
For it will tell you the way to joy, love and peace.

You will keep in perfect peace all who trust in you,
all whose thoughts are fixed on you! (Isaiah 26:3 NLT)

You are perfect to me my little child and
I know you very well.
I even know how many hairs
will be on your head and
whether they will be
black, yellow, brown or red.

But even the very hairs of your head are all numbered.
(Luke 12:7 KJV)

So never forget my dearest little one,
you have come into life,
and nothing will ever change this.
So, too, is my love for you,
a love that will forever be
one of absolute bliss.

Long ago the Lord said to Israel: "I have loved you,
my people, with an everlasting love. With unfailing love
I have drawn you to myself. (Jeremiah 31:3 NLT)

My word will teach you every good thing,
As you learn to love me
and love your neighbor
as yourself
for love is the master key.

"'Love the Lord your God with all your heart and with all your soul and with all your mind.' This is the first and greatest commandment. And the second is like it: 'Love your neighbor as yourself.' All the Law and the Prophets hang on these two commandments." (Matthew 22:37–39 NIV)

Finally, my little child, in the womb,
continue to listen to my words,
for they will refresh you
like the morning dew.
Remember them, speak them, and do them
for my love
will never leave you.
*Hugs and kisses forever to you. Your most
loving Dad, the Great I Am.*

My Word which goes from My mouth will not
return to Me empty. It will do what I want it to do and
will carry out My plan well. (Isaiah 55:11 NLV)

About the Authors

Phyllis Nicholas has been an educator for over 20 years. She has a deep love of helping others enjoy life to the fullest through the love, peace and joy of Jesus Christ. It is her hope that this book encourages parents to begin teaching God's wonderful words of life to the child in the womb and establishing a relationship for eternity with a loving God—even before birth.

Yes, God knew you before you were born and was thinking of you with everlasting love. You are a miracle who was meant to be here.

Anne Marie Wilson lives in Texas with her husband James Wilson. She and her sister, Phyllis continue to teach classes ministering to the child in the womb.

> "God's love for you began long before conception. What a joy and privilege to speak this Agape love to our future generations."

Printed in the USA
CPSIA information can be obtained
at www.ICGtesting.com
LVHW061250211123
764112LV00014B/655